Harmony Hustle for Women

Master the Art of Thriving in Life & Career

SaCola Lehr

Copyright © 2024 by SaCola Lehr

ISBN: 979-8-9990047-0-3

Book cover photo credit: Lady Iman Photography

DEDICATION

*For the woman who's tired of hustling harder
and ready to feel whole again.
This is your invitation back to yourself.*

CONTENTS

You Don't Have to Be Broken to Begin:

Hey there!

If you're reading this book, chances are you're managing a lot from career, raising kids, caregiving, or all of the above. And somewhere between the dishes and deadlines, you've asked yourself:

"Is it normal to feel this tired, this invisible?
"How can I juggle all these things without losing myself in the process?"
"Why does everyone else seem to manage things better than me?"

I want you to know something right away: **you're not broken…and you're not alone.**

This Book is for the Women Holding It Together

It's for the woman who shows up every day, even when she's exhausted. The one everyone relies on. The one surviving, but longing to thrive.

If you've ever thought, *"It's not bad enough for me to ask for help,"* I am giving you full-fledged permission to stop waiting for a crisis to happen before asking for support. You don't have to hit rock bottom to choose yourself. You don't have to shatter to shift. You definitely don't have to explain why you want more peace, joy, or me time.

There's an old saying that when people *know* better, they *do* better. What happens when we know better, yet still feel stuck? As Dr. Thema Bryant reminds us: *"You can know all the right things and still feel stuck. That's not failure-that's being a human."* This means sometimes, being human means recognizing that our weaknesses aren't holding us back; it's the invisible weight we've been carrying all along.

You're Not Broken. You're Carrying More Than You Know

At some point, every woman feels the frustration of knowing better, but not doing better. You've read books, journaled, gone to therapy, maybe even helped others. Yet when it comes to your own life? You stall. You procrastinate. You doom scroll on social media.

That resistance isn't laziness. It's the weight of years of societal and cultural conditioning telling us our needs should come last.

We've been taught for generations that selflessness is noble, and overextending ourselves is part of being a "good woman,". These cultural narratives didn't vanish with the right to vote or a seat at the table. They've gotten quieter… and sneakier.

Today, they show up as:

- Staying in toxic work environments because quitting feels like failure.
- Shrinking in relationships that drain us because we've been told to "make it work."
- Silencing our ambition because it might intimidate others.
- Pushing past exhaustion because rest feels like weakness.

These are prime examples of living in survival mode.

The Backpack Metaphor

Imagine you're standing at the base of a mountain with a backpack strapped on tight. You've mentally mapped out your route to ascend. You've cheered others on who have gone before you. Now it's your turn, but the weight of the backpack feels too heavy to climb.

You realize you're not just carrying supplies. You're carrying expectations, generational stories, guilt, and the pressure to "get it right." That invisible weight makes every step harder to take.

You Don't Need Another Push. You Need a Plan

You don't need more hustle. You need harmony.

This book is that plan. A guide to help you unpack what doesn't belong, lighten your load, and carry what matters with intention. Whether you're balancing career and caregiving, longing for the dreams yet lived, or craving more peace in your day, this is your moment.

We're not chasing perfection here. We're creating rhythm. It's about building a life that works with you, not against you.

Why I Wrote This Book

I didn't write *Harmony Hustle* because I've figured it all out. I wrote it because I've lived it. The burnout, overcommitment, and resentment, and I am still learning to recognize the signs before I crash.

This isn't a story from the finish line. It's a journal from the messy middle. I've walked the tightrope between ambition and exhaustion. I've been the "go-to" for everyone else while quietly asking, *"But who's here for me?"*

And when I dug deeper, I realized: what we call "burnout" in women isn't just about being busy, it's about feeling burdened. We inherited patterns that equate self-sacrifice with worth. But **self-sacrifice is not the same as self-worth.**

I wrote this book because I needed a different conversation, one that honored ambition and exhaustion, hope and healing, power and vulnerability. I felt that if I needed something like this, then maybe you do too.

What This Book Is and What It's Not

This is not another self-improvement book telling you to wake up at 5 a.m., color-code your calendar, and "manifest" balance while carrying the emotional weight of everyone around you, and you don't need a stricter routine.

This book is about doing less, but doing what matters. It's for the high-functioning woman who feels hollowed out. The one who smiles on teleconference calls but sighs from exhaustion off camera. The one praised for being "so strong," even while she's holding herself together with a hope and a prayer.

Here you'll find:

- Soulful questions and mindset shifts to reconnect to yourself
- Practical strategies that make space for both ambition and ease
- Permission to rest, reset, and resist the pressure to prove
- A compassionate framework that honors your humanity, not just your productivity

Because awareness without action leads to frustration, and action without alignment leads to burnout.

It's not about becoming someone new. It's about making space to be more of who you already are.

How to Read This Book

You don't have to start on page one. Each chapter is its own doorway. Enter where you need to.

Burned out? Start there.
Struggling with boundaries? Flip to that page.

This isn't a syllabus, it's a sanctuary. Read it with a highlighter or sneak in a few pages between meetings.

Go at your own pace.

A Glimpse of What's Possible

Beyond the calendar and caregiving, beneath the goals and quiet dreams, there's a voice whispering: *"There has to be a better way than just holding it all together."*

That whisper isn't just wishful thinking. It's wisdom. And this book is your invitation to listen.

You don't need to crash to course-correct.
You don't need to unravel to regroup.
You don't need to break down to start again.

Harmony isn't fictional. It's a return to yourself. A way of living that honors your goals and your nervous system. Your ambition and your well-being.

That's what it means to hustle with harmony.

It means stop waiting for permission, shrinking back, seeking approval, and managing a life that doesn't feel like yours.

It's time to Work it. Live it. Own it.

1

The Power to Begin Starts with the Harmony Within

"You can't pour from an empty cup. Take care of yourself first." – Unknown

Let's look at how society tells us what to do, and why it's okay to change those rules.

From a young age, many of us have felt the pressure to be nice, helpful, and agreeable. We learned to smile, fit in, and keep the peace, even when it meant ignoring our own needs. On the outside, we appeared fine. On the inside, we felt small.

We were praised for being selfless and caring, but rarely for being bold, audacious, setting boundaries, or daring to take up space. That's not by accident. For generations, women were taught to be quiet, grateful for what they have, and to measure their worth by how charitable they were. These lessons were repeated so often that they felt normal. They've been passed down like family heirlooms no one asked for, yet we still carry them today.

This is why so many capable, ambitious women hesitate when they want more. They shrink themselves. They stay in jobs, relationships, and routines that feel heavy because speaking up has been framed as arrogant, angry, or difficult. We were taught that wanting more was wrong. So, we settle for lives that look fine from the outside but feel exhausting inside.

It's not because we're weak. It's because we were never shown how to honor desires without guilt. That heaviness you carry? It's not failure, it's the tension between who you were told you ought to be and who you really are.

Here's the good news: you don't have to deconstruct your entire life to reclaim yourself. Change begins with one powerful question: *Who am I when I stop trying to be the person others expect me to be?*

The truth is, juggling work, family, and everything else can make you lose sight of yourself. When you're running on empty, everything feels challenging. However, when you make yourself a priority, you focus on what's important, and you unlock the freedom to succeed in your own way.

Sarah's Story to Whole Life Harmony

Everyone counted on Sarah.

She kept things afloat. She was punctual, ready to help whenever someone asked, and would often work late. Her boss trusted her. Her team relied on her. Since she looked so calm, no one thought to ask if she was okay or if she needed support.

At home, it was the same. Sarah was the one who organized everything. She meal prepped and remembered every special occasion. Despite feeling constantly tired, she was there to help others because Sarah believed, "That's what strong, resilient women do."

But here's what no one saw:

Behind her perfect emails and busy day, Sarah was falling apart. She woke up tired. She cried when no one was around. She kept telling herself to be thankful. Others had it worse, she thought. She had a good job and a loving family, so why wasn't she happy?

Her job paid well, so she stayed. She didn't want anyone to think she was complaining. Her relationship appeared fine, so she didn't change it. She thought asking for more would make people see her as selfish.

Then, one night, Sarah saw a picture on the fridge. Her youngest child had drawn it that day. It showed her family smiling in the sun, but Sarah was frowning.

She paused and realized that getting things done didn't matter if her child saw her as sad all the time. The drawing told the truth.

Sarah realized that her values did not align with her life.

She was aware that something needed to change.

She started by listing the things she did every day. After a week of doing this, she realized that work and chores took up the majority of her time. She was not taking time for herself, soccer matches, or family dinners.

Sarah requested assistance with her job. She told her boss that she wanted to pass on extra jobs to focus on more important tasks. Her boss didn't get angry. Instead, they appreciated Sarah's honesty.

From there, she drew a line in the sand.

Sarah set a firm 6 PM work stop. She turned off notifications after hours and over the weekend. And she added this simple line to her email signature:

> *"Thank you for reaching out. I'll respond during business hours, Monday through Friday, 9 AM to 6 PM. For urgent matters, please call me directly."*

On the home front, she began creating rituals, small but sacred. Tuesday became "Taco Night," where the family cooked and connected. Saturdays were for nature hikes and cheering from the sidelines. The moments weren't fancy, but they were hers and they were full of meaning.

The transformation wasn't instant, but it was lasting.

She wrestled with guilt in the beginning, worried she'd be seen as less driven or less dependable. But with time, she noticed the changes: more laughter, more focus, more peace. Her ideas at work were sharper. Her presence at home was deeper. Her energy? Finally, hers again.

And perhaps the most beautiful part?

Her courage created a ripple effect. Her boundaries gave others permission to set their own.

Her authenticity sparked conversations her coworkers didn't even know they needed.

All because she aligned her choices with what mattered most.

Lessons from Sarah's Story

Sarah didn't reinvent her entire life overnight.
She didn't run away or burn it all down.
She made intentional, courageous choices rooted in what mattered most to her.

Here's what her story teaches us:

- **Awareness is the first wake-up call.**
  Sometimes, it takes something small, a child's drawing, a sleepless night, a deep breath in the middle of the chaos to spark a moment of truth. That's not weakness. That's insight.

- **Your values are your moral compass.**
  When your choices no longer reflect what matters most, your body, your relationships, and your spirit will start to whisper, then scream for realignment.

- **Boundaries are not disrespectful.**
  When Sarah set clearer limits around her time, energy, and availability, she didn't lose respect she gained it.

- **Tiny changes lead to progress.**
  Taco nights, work curfews, a revised email signature. These aren't grand gestures, but they are bold ones. They signal a shift from surviving to living with intention.

- **Maintaining your peace is powerful.**

  When you honor your own capacity, others take notice, and sometimes, they start doing the same. Your harmony can create healing beyond yourself.

From Awareness to Action: Tools to Reclaim Your Priorities

Sarah's story isn't rare. In fact, it's more common than we realize. So many women feel stuck, not because they're lazy or unmotivated, but because no one ever taught us how to live in alignment with our values while still showing up for everything (and everyone) that matters.

It's not about overhauling your entire life overnight. It's about starting small, with intention. One moment. One decision. One new rhythm at a time.

Let's begin with what's already yours: your time, your energy, your voice.

You're More Than a Title

Let's get real: you are more than your job description.
You're a caregiver. A partner. A friend. A mentor. A daughter.
These roles are meaningful, but they will deplete you if you never stop to ask: *What do I need?*
The answer doesn't have to be complicated. Here are a few simple but powerful ways to begin reclaiming your priorities.

1. The Morning Ritual Reset

You don't need a 5 a.m. miracle routine. Just ten minutes.

Light a candle.
Sip your coffee slowly.
Write down one thing you're grateful for.
Stretch.
Breathe.

And just be before the demands begin.

→ **Try This:** Use the Insight Timer app for guided mindfulness to start your morning with calm and clarity.

2. The 3 P's Method

This is a quick and practical way to focus on what truly matters. Each morning or evening, list your top priorities under the following:

- **Personal:** (e.g., Exercise, drink water, therapy session)
- **Professional:** (e.g., Prep client deck, respond to key email)
- **People:** (e.g., Check in with a friend, attend your kid's recital)

When everything feels urgent, this tool helps you remember what's truly important.

Quick Questions, Real Answers

These are the questions I hear most from smart, capable women who are doing so much and still wondering if it's okay to want more ease.

Q1: How do I prioritize myself without feeling selfish?

→ *By realizing that it's not selfish, it's strategic.* Think of an oxygen mask on an airplane: if you can't breathe, you can't help anyone else. Start with 10–15 minutes a day just for you.

Quick Tip: Use that time for a ritual, reflection, or simply sipping your coffee without multitasking.

Q2: How do I identify my priorities when everything feels urgent?

→ Ask yourself: *What actually matters long-term?*
Break it down using the **3 Ps method**. Focus on what aligns with your core values, not just what's loudest.

Q3: What if I don't have time to focus on myself?

→ You do. But you might be giving it away.
Time-block. Delegate. Let go of the non-essential. Even 5 minutes of intention is a powerful start.

Quick Tip: Protect your peace like it's your paycheck, because it is.

Q4: How do I stop feeling guilty about putting my needs first?

→ Guilt often comes from outdated conditioning. Flip the script: caring for yourself teaches others how to care for themselves, too.

Quick Tip: Self-care isn't indulgence, it's inner leadership.

Q5: How do I avoid burnout when I feel stretched too thin?

→ Burnout isn't always loud. Sometimes, it's just numbness. The key is rebalancing your input and output. Take breaks. Rest without apologizing.

Quick Tip: Each week, delegate one thing and say "no" to another.

Q6: What do I do when my priorities conflict with each other?

→ Start with what's most *urgent* and *important*.
In Chapter 3, we'll dig deeper into a powerful decision tool called the **Priority Matrix,** a simple way to sort what truly matters and what can wait.

Quick Tip: Don't aim for perfection. Aim for progress with peace.

REFLECTION QUESTION

What's one small way you can put yourself first this week?

Final Thoughts: Finding the Harmony Within

You don't need to change everything overnight. You just need to *begin* with one decision, one pause, one new boundary.

Harmony isn't about perfection. It's about the permission to honor your values, listen to your body, and protect your energy.

When you fill your own cup first, everything else begins to flow.

You've got this. You're not alone.

2

Let Values Steer
the Way Clear

"No one knows what you're worth but you."
-Pearl Bailey

Have you ever said "yes" to something and immediately felt that pit-in-your-stomach regret? Or kept a commitment you knew deep down wasn't right for you, but you didn't want to rock the boat? Yep, me too. That uneasy feeling is usually your inner compass trying to tell you something, your core values are out of sync.

Before we talk about strategy, goals, or boundaries, we need to talk about *values*. Your values are your home base. When life gets busy, messy, or downright overwhelming, they bring you back to what matters most. And when you make choices from that place, it doesn't just feel good, it *is* good.

Let's break it down.

What Are Core Values?

Core values are the most important rules you live by. They are your beliefs that help you make choices every day. These beliefs help you know what is right for you. They help you stay true to yourself and your actions.

Think of them as your internal GPS. When you're honoring them, life flows. When you're ignoring them, life feels off, even if everything looks "successful" from the outside.

Some common values include:

- Integrity
- Freedom
- Compassion
- Creativity
- Connection
- Growth
- Simplicity

Your values are unique to you. They aren't trendy or borrowed from someone else's vision board. They're personal, powerful, and practical.

Why Core Values Matter in Work and Life

When your values are clear, you stop wasting time chasing what doesn't belong to you. You stop overcommitting, overperforming, and overexplaining. Instead, you start showing up with purpose, clarity, and confidence.

Core values help you:

- Make aligned decisions
- Set boundaries that feel good
- Stay motivated and focused
- Avoid burnout by staying true to what energizes you

Let's say one of your top values is *flexibility*. That means a rigid work schedule might slowly drain you. Or maybe your top value is *authenticity,* so anytime you're forced to code-switch, mask, or fit into a mold, it chips away at your energy.

Knowing your values lets you name what's not working and, more importantly, change it.

Living in Alignment

Alignment isn't about being perfect. It's about making decisions that honor your values more often than not. You won't always get it right, and that's okay. But knowing your values gives you something to come back to.

And when you *do* get it right, that's when the enlightenment happens. Your energy feels cleaner. Your choices feel lighter. And the outcome feels a whole lot more like you. I talk about this in Episode 13 of my podcast, *Work It, Live It, Own It!* The episode is called **"Core Values in Action: How Harmony Between Life and Work Drives Success,"** and it dives into how discovering and living by your values can change not just how you work, but how you live.

The Core Value Exercise

Here's one of my favorite clarity tools.

Ask **25 people** you know, like, and trust to give you **three adjectives** that describe you. These can be family, friends, co-workers, mentors, or anyone who's known you for a while.

1. Look for patterns. Are words like "creative," "thoughtful," or "driven" showing up again and again?
2. Circle the ones that *resonate* with you.
3. Pick 5–7 that feel like your core. These might just be your values in disguise.

Next, write out what those values *look like* when you're at your best. For example:

- **Creativity**: I give myself time and space to think outside the box in my work.
- **Compassion**: I speak kindly to myself and others, even on the worst days.
- **Integrity**: I follow through, even when no one's watching.

This step grounds your values in your real, everyday life. That's how values become a compass, not just a Pinterest quote.

Aligning Values with Boundaries

Now that you've got your core values, boundaries become clearer.

In Chapter 4, I talk about how boundaries aren't walls; they're bridges. And values? They're the blueprint for building those bridges.

If you value peace, then you'll probably need boundaries around your time and energy. If you value growth, maybe you need boundaries around relationships or environments that keep you small.

Values help you say a powerful *yes* to what serves you and a confident *no* to what doesn't.

Here are Some Takeaways

Your values aren't just a list of nice words. They are your filter, your foundation, and your freedom. When you live by them, you don't just hustle, you *honor* your life.

You deserve that kind of clarity. That kind of power. That kind of harmony.

So, go ahead. Discover your values. Define them. Live them. And own every step of your journey.

Because the life you want? Start with what you value most.

3

Find Your Flow in Work and Life, then Watch it Grow

"Life isn't about balance; it's about making everything work together."
- Michelle Obama

I've learned that life isn't about perfectly balancing time between work and home. It's about creating a rhythm that works for you, one that adapts to what life asks of you without leaving you exhausted and scattered.

This chapter is here to help you shape a flow that blends your work, caregiving, and personal time in a way that supports *you*. Because work-life harmony isn't about strict lines or ideal schedules, it's about synergy. Some days, your career may need more of you. On other days, your family or your own well-being might take center stage. And that's not a failure, it's real life.

Meet Keisha and How She Found Her Flow.

Keisha, a high achiever, worked as a corporate trainer; her days were filled with leading workshops, mentoring professionals, and traveling for client engagements. Suddenly, life took a sharp turn. Her mother was diagnosed with early-stage dementia, and Keisha became her primary caregiver.

Every morning, she'd wake up early to make breakfast for her mom. By 8 a.m., she would log onto her computer, facilitating back-to-back sessions until late afternoon. Evenings were a blur, completing medical paperwork and juggling household chores.

Yet, Keisha held on to her dream of building her consulting side business into something full-time. Most nights, she'd open her laptop to write blog content, plan outreach, or explore partnerships, but exhaustion would take over. She'd often fall asleep at her desk, only to wake up with aching shoulders, an untouched to-do list, and a fresh wave of guilt.

The Breaking Point

One Wednesday morning, Keisha felt an indescribable pang of anxiety. That nagging feeling of "I'm forgetting something" wouldn't go away.

Midway through a presentation, she received a text message with a notification letting her know that she missed her mother's medical appointment. Her heart sank, because it was at that moment she realized not only did she miss her mother's appointment, she'd also missed a deadline for a critical report for a client. By the afternoon, her manager emailed her to follow up. That night, everything came crashing down on her.

She could no longer hold back the tears. "I can't keep living like this," she confided to her best friend, "I feel like I'm failing at everything: my work, my mom, and my own dreams."

Taking Control Redefined

We often think "taking control" means holding it all together, handling everything on our plate. However, that's not what real control looks like. It's about choosing what's most important and letting everything else fall into place.

Keisha knew something had to change. That weekend, she gave herself permission to pause. She reflected on her priorities, researched time management tools, and, perhaps most importantly, she stopped trying to power through alone.

She Asked for Help

Keisha realized that she couldn't keep pouring from an empty cup. She picked up the phone and called her siblings. They started a weekly video chat to check in and share updates on their mom's care. Then she hired a part-time caregiver through Visiting Angels. That one decision freed up two evenings a week, allowing her to run her consulting business.

Permission reminder: Asking for help doesn't mean you're failing. It means you're human and wise enough to know that doing it alone isn't sustainable.

She Reorganized Her Days

Instead of letting things become a blur, Keisha started creating a daily rhythm. She blocked time off for things that mattered most with a time-focused schedule.

Mornings: Major work-big projects, client reports, or anything that requires focus.

- **Afternoons:** Client calls and caregiving tasks
- **Evenings (twice a week):** Time for her consulting business and creative ideas.

This gave Keisha some breathing room. Each part of her day had its own section, allowing her space to catch up.

She Let Technology Lighten the Load

Keisha let her phone carry some of the weight instead of keeping everything in her head. She synced all caregiving appointments in her Google Calendar and set reminders. Technology didn't solve every problem, but it kept her from missing appointments.

She Conserved Her Energy

Learning that her energy was worth protecting was the hardest transition to make. Keisha started saying no to low-priority tasks. She reminded her corporate clients of her work availability. She stopped explaining to people her reasons behind certain decisions and started honoring her limits. She discovered that boundaries weren't about shutting people out. They were about giving herself room to breathe and space to show up optimally in the places that mattered.

The Breakthrough

A few weeks into her new approach to life, Keisha noticed positive changes. Her mom's care was more consistent. Her corporate clients noticed the improvement in communication. She even had time, real, focused time, to work on her consulting business without feeling like she was stealing it from somewhere else.

But the biggest shift?
Here's what Keisha said about being compassionate with herself.

"I realized I don't have to do things perfectly. What matters is that I'm doing my best and building a life that actually works for me."

Takeaway

Keisha's story is a reminder that harmony isn't a dream. It's completely doable. When we ask for help, plan our days with intention, and protect our energy with clear boundaries, we move beyond survival mode. We make room to actually thrive.

How to Find Your Flow

Here are some strategies to help you create a sustainable rhythm:

Batch Tasks by Energy Levels:
Structure your day in a way that honors your natural rhythms:

- **Morning:** Focused, strategic tasks (proposals, writing, deep thinking)

- **Afternoon:** Light tasks like emails, errands, or creative planning

- **Evening:** Household tasks, family time, or rest

Build in Buffer Time
Life doesn't run on a perfect schedule. Add 15 to 30 minute buffers between meetings or transitions so unexpected delays don't derail your entire day.

Delegate with Confidence
Let go of the guilt that comes with asking for help it's a critical step in creating more breathing room for yourself, both at work and at home.

- **At work:** Delegate recurring tasks or low-priority responsibilities to colleagues or a virtual assistant. To set them up for success, create a detailed SOP manual or video tutorial that shows how you accomplish the task. This way, you're providing clear instructions and making it easier for others to deliver quality work.

- **At home:** Hire help for cleaning, caregiving, or errands when you can. Tools like Care.com for finding trustworthy caregiving help or TaskRabbit for tackling errands can be great starting points.

- **Accepting "good enough" is okay.**
  If you ask a family member or a roommate to help with chores, adjust to how they do things. It may not be exactly how you would do it, and that's okay. Everything is not meant to be under your control, and nothing is perfect.

Delegation doesn't just save you time; it allows you to focus on what truly matters. But it takes patience and practice. The more you create space for others to help, and the more you accept their efforts, the closer you move toward a harmonious flow between work and life, and you're allowing them to show up and share the load with you in their own way.

The Importance of Community Support

You're not alone and you're certainly not the only one navigating this season in life. Seeking help and leaning into community can make all the difference when you're trying to balance work, life, and caregiving responsibilities.

Tap into the power of your community by finding others who understand your struggles. It can be a game-changer. Seeking support doesn't just lighten the load; it reminds you that your feelings and challenges are valid, and that help is available.

If you need support taking care of an older loved one, here are a few places to start:

- **AARP Caregiving Resources:** Offers free tools, guides, and education for family caregivers.

- **Alzheimer's Association:** Provides support groups, helplines, and resources for families caring for loved ones.

FINAL THOUGHTS
on Finding Your Flow

Work-life harmony isn't about juggling two separate worlds. It's about weaving them together on your own terms.

Progress isn't found in perfection. It's found in the small, intentional shifts you make every day.

- Start with what matters most.
- Protect your energy like it's sacred, because it is.
- Let support in. Let guilt out.

Remember, your life doesn't need to look like anyone else's version of success to feel deeply aligned with your values. You are part of a larger network of people navigating similar pains, struggles, and setbacks, and many of them found their way through resilience, persistence, and support.

We'll explore more on this topic in Chapter Seven, where we will discover how having a supportive community is a vital tool for finding harmony, gaining clarity, and shaping your work-life narrative.

In Chapter Four, we'll dive into a tool that helps you prioritize your time and tasks based on urgency and importance. When you start to focus on what truly deserves your energy, it can be a total game-changer.

REFLECTION QUESTION:

What's one responsibility you can delegate or release this week?

Once you have identified it, take action and give it time to work.

You've got this, and you're exactly where you need to be to begin.

4

Smart Moves for Your Boundary Setting Groove

"Daring to set boundaries is about having the courage to love ourselves, even when we risk disappointing others."
— Brené Brown

If it took us years to grow into adulthood, then finding your harmonious groove will take time. The reality check is that work-life harmony isn't just about inspiration and motivation. It's about moving with purpose and intention.

You don't have to hustle harder to achieve harmony in your life. You need a plan and the aspirations to act. This chapter will help you with the mindset shifts and strategies you need to keep you aligned when life starts to feel out of whack. We're going to dive into some real-life systems and habits that can help you manage your time, conserve your energy, protect your peace, while staying connected to what truly matters.

Setting Boundaries: Educating People on How to Treat You Right

Boundaries help you connect with the people and priorities that matter without losing yourself in the process.

Don't think of boundaries as a strong fortified wall that blocks others from getting access to you. They're more like a red velvet rope at a party. You let people in as long as they agree to your rules. When you create boundaries in your career and personal life, you protect your time and feelings.

Setting boundaries isn't just about saying no; it's about confidently saying yes to what aligns with your values, well-being, and purpose. When you find yourself feeling like the weight of the world is on your shoulders, here is a boundary manifesto I want to share with you.

The Boundaries Manifesto

You are not being selfish. You are being wise.
You are not failing anyone. You are showing others what
self-respect looks like.
You are not meant to carry other people's burdens alone.
You are meant to live, love, and lead in a way that allows
you to flourish and thrive.

The Workplace Tightrope

Navigating boundaries in the workplace is like walking a tightrope. If we lean too far on either side, we can become ultra-compliant or excessively rigid. One of the smartest yet hardest moves we can make is setting boundaries.

At work, boundaries are often the first thing to go when we want to be seen as dependable, committed, or "a team player." We work overtime and take on last-minute projects. We cover for others and respond to emails after hours. Let's be honest: we've all been there. Your boss drops a new project on your desk when you're already overloaded with work. Perhaps you run your own business, and a client gives you a task with zero notice and expects spectacular results. You might feel the pressure to smile, nod, and "make it work."

The best thing we can do in situations like this is to back up, breathe, and be quiet. Take a deep breath, listen intently, and ask clarifying questions to assess what's realistic. Sometimes it means having the courage to say, *"That sounds like a great idea! If we want this task to be successful, I will need more time or additional help. Perhaps we can adjust some expectations."*

Designate Clear Work Hours

For example, if your workday ends at 6:00 PM, honor that time. Close the laptop. Turn off your phone notifications. Allow yourself to transition into your personal life. This small shift allows your nervous system to reset, and it tells your brain and your loved ones that you deserve restoration, too.

Communicate with Clarity and Confidence

Let others know what to expect. Whether it's using an auto-responder to manage email expectations or gently reminding your team of your availability, clear communication prevents resentment and builds respect.

The Cost of People-Pleasing

The cost of always saying yes is steep. It often leads to resentment, burnout, and a slow erosion of your confidence. Each time you override your emotional and physical bandwidth, you're sending a message to yourself that your personal well-being doesn't matter and is negotiable.

People-pleasing also presents us with a unique challenge. When we're at work, if we voice our opinion and advocate for ourselves, and it goes against the company's culture, we could potentially be labeled as "difficult," "not a team player," or "too emotional."

In our personal lives, if we ask for support, we may feel like we're "failing" as a wife, mother, or daughter, because we've internalized the myth that being strong means being able to do it all without ever needing a break or support. That's not strength. That's self-abandonment.

Courageous Conversations at Home

Setting boundaries doesn't just apply to your career; it's critical at home as well. If you're living with your family or a roommate, and you've become the default cook, cleaner, and homework helper. You weren't meant to carry the load of household chores by yourself. Schedule a time when you are not emotionally charged and have a conversation. Ask for help. Be clear about what you want and need. Here are some conversation starters.

- "Can we divide the chores so we all have time to recharge?"
- "I need help with dinner three nights a week."
- "I'd love to help, but I have other commitments that require my attention."

Taking Care of Aging Parents

Another layer of personal boundary-setting is taking care of aging parents. Many women in the "sandwich generation" are not only raising children and working full-time jobs, but also supporting their parents emotionally, physically, and sometimes financially.

This is where the heartache can really hit the hardest.

Loving and caring for your family is a beautiful gift. But not when it comes at the cost of your own health, financial security, or sense of self.

You are allowed to say: "I want to be here for you, but I also need to protect my own stability." You are allowed to set limits even with people you love the most.

Prioritize with Purpose, Delegate with Confidence

When everything feels urgent, nothing actually gets your best version of you. The key to working smarter is deciding what truly deserves your time and getting help with the rest.

Here are a few strategies you can try.

Create a Weekly Priority Plan

At the start of each week, you can make a list of your tasks and sort them by urgency and importance. Focus on the tasks that will move the needle, not just the ones screaming the loudest. A simple tool like the Eisenhower/Priority Matrix (coming up later in this chapter) can help.

Delegate or Outsource (Without Guilt)

You don't have to do it all.

- For errands, explore tools like TaskRabbit
- For caregiving support, try Care.com or a local respite program
- For home management, lean on grocery delivery or cleaning services

Here's your delegation permission slip. If you choose to delegate a task or chore, it doesn't mean you're dropping the ball. It means you're protecting your peace and conserving your energy for more important things.

Protect the Most Important Asset, You

Self-care isn't a reward after checking everything off your to-do list; it's what keeps you strong to show up for the list in the first place.

Think of it this way: *you're the asset.* And every asset needs protection to stay valuable.

Here are two strategies to try:

Make Appointments with Yourself and Keep Them

Treat your well-being like a non-negotiable rendezvous with yourself. Block out time in your calendar for what refuels you. It could be a walk, a quiet cup of tea or coffee, journaling, or even a short dance break between meetings.

Keep It Simple, Keep It Steady

You don't need a full spa day to reset. Even a daily 15-minute pause can create a powerful ripple effect for your emotional and mental well-being. Consistency is what makes the biggest difference.

Three Habits for Daily Harmony

Let's zoom in on three practices that can add flow and ease to your days:

1. **Cultivate a Support System**
   Let people in. Let them help.
   Support lightens the load of doing everything alone.

2. **Embrace Flexibility with Structure**
   Harmony needs both stability and flexibility. Create routines that serve you, but also give yourself permission to adjust without guilt when life shifts.

3. **Practice the End-of-Day Unplug Ritual**
   Your brain needs time to power down and recharge. Set a boundary between your work and rest. Whether it's shutting your laptop, taking a walk, or silencing notifications, your mind and body will thank you.

Tools for Smarter Moves: The Priority Matrix

Also known as the Eisenhower Matrix, it divides tasks into:

▶ **Urgent & Important**: Do now

▶ **Not Urgent but Important**: Plan for later

▶ **Urgent but Not Important:** Delegate

▶ **Not Urgent nor Important**: Eliminate

This one tool can save you hours of energy each week.

Urgent	Not Urgent
Important	**Important**
Quadrant 1: DO NOW	**Quadrant 2: PLAN FOR LATER**
Tasks to complete immediately.	Tasks to schedule for later.
Example: Client deadline today.	Example: Planning next quarter's goals.
Not Important	**Not Important**
Quadrant 3: DELEGATE	**Quadrant 4: ELIMINATE**
Tasks to assign to others.	Tasks to let go of completely.
Example: Routine emails.	Example: Excessive social media.

Lessons from Emma's Story: From Burnout to Harmony

Emma, a project manager and mom of two, felt like life was a blur. Her evenings consisted of answering work messages, reheated dinners, and bedtime routines.

She was showing up for everyone…except herself.

Her turning point came one night at bedtime, when she realized she hadn't made eye contact with her daughter all day. That moment ignited a spark within her.

Here's how she got her harmonious groove back:

1. **She Set Clear Boundaries**
    Emma told her team about her new working hours and created a log-off ritual at 6 PM. It felt uncomfortable at first, but within two weeks, her evenings felt like hers again.

2. **She Prioritized and Delegated**
    Using the priority matrix, she batched tasks and gave admin work to a virtual assistant. That one move added hours back to her each week.

3. **She Practiced Self-Care Without Guilt**
    Three mornings a week, she carved out "Emma Time." No emails. No chores. Just space to breathe.

4. **She Built a Support System**
    Emma joined a group for working moms. The community offered tips, encouragement, and permission to relax.

5. **She Embraced Flexibility**

When her son got sick, she shifted her schedule instead of letting things spiral out of control. She honored her nurturing role as a mother and ditched the guilt.

REFLECTION:
Your Turn to Shift

Let Emma's story and your own insight be the nudge to a fresh start.

What boundary can you set this week?

What task can you delegate or release?

What type of support can you lean on right now?

Key Takeaways: Smart Moves for a Harmonious Groove

Set Boundaries: Define clear lines between work and personal life.

Prioritize Self-Care: Treat your well-being as a non-negotiable.

Use the Priority Matrix: Work smarter, not harder.

Cultivate Support: Connection makes the load lighter.

Embrace Flexibility: Life shifts, your schedule can, too.

ACTION
Steps

Choose *one* step to put in motion this week:

- ▶ **Set a Clear Boundary:** Log off at a set time or create a shutdown ritual.

- ▶ **Use the Priority Matrix:** Delegate or delete two nonessential tasks.

- ▶ **Schedule Self-Care:** Block 15 minutes for something just for you.

FINAL
THOUGHTS on
Finding Your Groove

You don't need a life overhaul to create harmony.
Just one aligned choice at a time.

Each small shift you make is proof that you're building your own version of a harmonious life, one that feels deeply your own.

5

Time is on Your Side – Tools to Help You Thrive

"Time is what we want most, but what we use worst."
- William Penn

Time mastery isn't about squeezing more into your day; it's about focusing on what truly matters and using your energy with intention. In this chapter, you'll discover strategies to take control of your time, boost your productivity, and create a life that feels both purposeful and fulfilling.

First, let me tell you about Rachel, a marketing consultant and mom of three. At one point, she was stretched so thin that every day felt like survival mode. Her journey from burnout to balance proves that mastering your time isn't just possible, it's transformative.

Rachel's Breaking Point

Rachel had always dreamt of writing a book. A typical day consisted of client meetings, helping with homework, and endless to-do lists. Her dream sat untouched at the bottom of every planner page.

She was always in reactive mode. Even when she had an hour free to herself, she didn't know where to begin. She felt like she was running in circles. Always busy but never moving towards her goal.

One evening, she stared at the blinking cursor on her screen while her children were playing downstairs. She couldn't take it anymore. She knew something had to change. With the help of a friend and an accountability partner, she began to implement some strategies. Here's what she did.

Step 1: Prioritize with Purpose

Rachel started mapping out her tasks using the Priority Matrix:

- **Urgent & Important:** Finalizing a campaign launch for a major client.
- **Important but Not Urgent:** Outlining her book chapters.
- **Urgent but Not Important:** Non-essential emails.
- **Neither Urgent nor Important:** Late-night scrolling on social media.

Rachel soon realized her dream of writing a book was trapped under the "Important but Not Urgent" quadrant. So she dedicated early mornings to writing. Routine tasks were shifted to later in the day.

She stopped letting the urgent things take over the important ones. That one change shifted her dream to reality.

Step 2: Structure for Flow, Not Just Function

Instead of a scattered schedule, Rachel created a simple rhythm to her days:

- **Morning: Mind and Movement**
  Journaling and a short walk before the kids woke up, and two mornings for writing.

- **Midday: Deep Work & Dream Building**
  Client work

- **Evening: Connection and Creativity**
  Technology-free dinners, family time, and rediscovering her love for painting.

She used to think every minute had to be productive. Now, she understands that rest and joy are productive too.

Step 3: Work in Focus Blocks

Rachel dreaded long writing sessions until she tried the **Pomodoro Technique:** 25 minutes of focused work, no multitasking, five minutes of rest time.

By breaking her time up, writing felt less intimidating. Before she knew it, she had written two chapters.

Step 4: Embrace Life's Curveballs

When her youngest child's school closed unexpectedly, Rachel didn't panic. She adjusted her schedule. She moved her writing to the evening and gave herself grace. She began to see time not as an enemy but as an ally. Her productivity increased, but most importantly, her stress and anxiety decreased.

Identify What Matters Most

To begin, it's essential to identify what's truly important. When you reflect on your goals and values, you can intentionally align your daily activities with what matters most. Instead of feeling swept up in the whirlwind of endless tasks, you'll learn how to create space for what genuinely lights you up.

1. Prioritize Tasks Effectively

Not all tasks carry the same weight, and understanding how to prioritize ensures your energy is spent on high-impact activities.

One effective tool is the Eisenhower/Priority Matrix, which divides tasks into four categories:

- **Urgent and Important:** Tasks requiring immediate attention.
- **Important but Not Urgent:** Tasks that move you closer to long-term goals.
- **Urgent but Not Important:** Tasks you can delegate.
- **Not Urgent nor Important:** Tasks to eliminate entirely.

2. Boost Focus with the Pomodoro Technique

Sometimes, the secret to accomplishing more lies in working smarter, not harder. The Pomodoro Technique is a fantastic way to break work into manageable chunks of focus and rest.

Here's how it works: Spend 25 minutes fully immersed in a task, then take a 5-minute break. After completing four cycles, reward yourself with a longer 20–30-minute break. Feel free to tweak the timing to suit your needs.

It's effective because:

- It helps prevent burnout by pacing your efforts.
- It keeps your energy and focus steady throughout the day.

Getting started is simple:

- Use an app like Forest or a basic timer to track your sessions.
- Commit to focusing on one task per interval to maximize productivity.

3. Structure Your Day Like A Pro

I had the pleasure of speaking with digital nomad and coach Jermane Cheatham on my podcast, *Work It, Live It, Own It!* episode 54. He shared a straightforward yet transformative framework for dividing your day into three purposeful segments:

- **Morning (6:00 a.m. to 8:00 a.m.): Self-Care** Begin your day with activities that ground and energize you, whether that's exercising, practicing mindfulness, journaling, or simply enjoying quiet reflection.

- **Midday (8:00 a.m. to 12:00 p.m.): Money-Making Tasks** Dedicate these peak energy hours to revenue-generating activities or high-impact work.

- **Evening (12:00 p.m. to 8:00 p.m.): Life-Enriching Activities** Use this time to nurture relationships, explore personal growth, or engage in hobbies that bring you joy.

4. Leverage Technology to Stay Organized

Let's face it, life can get busy, but the right tools can help you stay on top of it all. Apps and technology are excellent allies in simplifying your workflow and keeping you organized.

Here are a few favorites:

- **Trello:** Perfect for visualizing projects and tracking progress.

- **Toggl:** A simple tool to monitor how you spend your time.

- **Evernote:** Keep all your notes and ideas in one handy place.

Pro Tip: Experiment with a few tools to see which fit your workflow best. There's no one-size-fits-all solution.

5. Adapt to Real-Life Disruptions + Flexible Mindset Strategy

Life is rarely predictable, but a flexible mindset can be your anchor when unexpected challenges arise.

Flexibility doesn't have to feel like failure; make it a part of your daily rhythm.

Here's how to embrace this principle:

- **Assess & Adapt:** Before reacting to a new demand, ask, "Is this truly urgent?"
- **Build in Buffer Time:** Leave space in your schedule for curveballs and surprises.

Reflection: What Can You Learn from Rachel?

Her story is a reminder that time mastery doesn't start with apps or timers; it begins with clarity, courage, and commitment to what truly matters.

Ask yourself:

- Are you protecting time for your most meaningful goals?
- Is your current schedule a reflection of your values or your stress?
- What's one shift you can make today to feel more in control?

Summary of Key Points

- **Prioritize Tasks:** Use the Priority Matrix to cut through the noise and distractions.

- **Create Daily Structure:** Match your energy to the right tasks at the appropriate time.

- **Focus in Chunks:** Techniques like Pomodoro help keep your momentum steady.

- **Leverage Technology:** Streamline your workflow with apps such as Trello or Toggl.

- **Structure Your Day:** Create intentional rhythms of self-care, productive work, and enrichment.

- **Embrace Flexibility:** Disruptions happen; respond with flexibility, not guilt.

REFLECTION QUESTIONS

- Are you protecting your time with meaningful goals?

- Does your current schedule reflect your values or your stress?

- What's one shift you can make this week to feel more in control?

ACTIONABLE
Steps

1. **Create Your Matrix:** Sort this week's tasks into four quadrants using the Priority Matrix (See Chapter 4 for an example)

2. **Try the Pomodoro Technique:** Commit to one 25-minute focused session today.

3. **Restructure Your Day:** Align morning, afternoons, and evenings with what fuels you.

4. **Experiment with Tools:** Test apps like Trello, Toggl, or Forest to simplify your workflow.

FINAL
THOUGHTS on
Time Mastery

Time mastery isn't about perfection; it's about progress, one intentional choice at a time.

Rachel didn't write her book overnight. But with every boundary, every Pomodoro, and every mindful "no," she turned overwhelm into momentum.

By prioritizing what truly matters, focusing your energy where it counts, and remaining flexible when challenges arise, you can stay consistent. Remember, each step you take is proof you're building a life that aligns with your deepest values!

6

Check on You, Before You Push Through

"Take care of your body. It's the only place you have to live."
– Jim Rohn

As women, we're taught to push through. We keep moving past the deadlines, family logistics, careers, pain, and fatigue. We silence health ailments with a pill, another coffee/energy drink, or a resigned "I'll deal with it later." We wear reliability and perseverance like a badge of honor. The problem is that the badge can hang like a noose around our necks.

It costs too much to maintain the "push through" mentality. Many women learn to rest only after a health crisis forces them to. For some, rest comes too late. Some women say, "I just need to lie down," and they never wake up. This is not a dramatic image; it's a warning we can't afford to ignore.

In this chapter, we'll get blunt about what it means to prioritize health, not when everything else is handled, but now. Wellness is not a luxury. It's not optional. It's the foundation that allows you to live, lead, love, and thrive.

What You'll Learn

- Why pushing through pain can be dangerous

- How to recognize subtle signs your body needs care

- The importance of medical self-advocacy

- What to say (and ask) when medical providers or employers dismiss.

- Questions to ask your doctor or care team

- Practical steps to take care of loved ones without burning out.

Your Story: The Power of Speaking Up

In **episode 64 of the *It's a Hard No* podcast**, I shared one of the scariest and most transformative moments of my life. I was in real excruciating pain. Something felt deeply wrong. I almost dismissed it, and nearly "pushed through" like I always had.

Thankfully, I didn't. I listened to my body. I advocated for my rights to a medical examination despite pushback from my doctor. I got the care and treatment I need, including life-saving surgeries. When I took time off from work to recover, my director criticized me for being out of work for six weeks. Instead of compassion, I met scrutiny. As if needing to heal was a problem, and my life wasn't precious and sacred.

This isn't just my story; it's systemic. From medical professionals who minimize symptoms to workplaces that reward burnout, the message is loud and clear: "Get over it and get back to work." Here's the truth: you are not overreacting. You are not weak. You don't have to earn the right to rest.

Advocate for Yourself Even When It's Uncomfortable

When you walk into a medical appointment, you have the right to ask questions, request tests, and seek second opinions. It's your body, be an active participant in its care.

Questions to Ask Your Healthcare Provider:

- How do you include patients in decisions about their care?
- What experience do you have with patients who share my symptoms?
- What additional tests can we run to rule things out?
- If tests are "normal," but I still feel unwell, what's our plan?
- Are you open to a second opinion if needed?
- How can we communicate after this visit (email, portal, phone)?

Red Flags to watch for when meeting with a medical provider:

- Dismissing or interrupting you.
- Saying "You're just stressed" without further explanation.
- Using condescending or fear-based language.
- Getting defensive when you ask questions.

You are not "difficult" for seeking clarity. You are responsible.

How to Talk to an Unsympathetic Employer

If you face pushback at work, there's no need to be combative or defensive. Be clear and professional. Here's an example: *"Hi _____, I'm currently managing a health issue that requires treatment and recovery time. I'm committed to my work; here's the plan to keep things moving: [brief plan, coverages, expected return]. I will keep you updated and stay reachable for urgent matters. I appreciate your support while I get the care I need."*

Caring for a Loved One: Treat Advocacy Like a Job

When you're a caregiver, compassion alone won't be enough. You need a strategy and documentation.

What helped me and my family members during the months of hospital transfers was keeping a notebook handy, where I recorded:

- Medication names and doses.
- Notes from doctors' rounds.
- Any changes in condition.
- Names of the nurses or aides on duty
- Dates and times of incidents.

When I did this, some medical personnel were taken aback. Others were grateful. One nurse told me, *"Thank you. Records don't always get updated quickly enough during transfers, so this helps more than you know."* That notebook became my proof, my record, my accountability partner.

If you're in this season, consider:

- Keep a dedicated care journal
- Ask for care meetings
- Request a patient advocate or case manager
- Trust your gut and speak up when something feels off
- Don't go alone, bring a trusted family member or friend

You are part of the care team. Your voice matters.

JOURNAL
Prompt

Pause and reflect for five minutes:

- What signs has your body been giving you lately that you've ignored or minimized

- What would it look like to honor your health *before* it becomes a crisis?

Final
THOUGHT

You can't pour from an empty cup, and you cannot fulfill your calling if your body is breaking down. True strength isn't in "powering through," it's in pausing, noticing, and choosing care over chaos.

You deserve to feel well. You deserve to be heard. You deserve to rest without guilt.

Self-care is not selfish. Self-advocacy is not rude.
It's how we survive and thrive for the people and the purpose we love.

7

Build Your Tribe That's on Your Side

*"Alone we can do so little; together
we can do so much."
- Helen Keller*

Why You Can't Do This Alone

Work-life harmony doesn't happen in isolation. It's shaped by the people around you, the ones who listen when you need to vent, cheer you on when you succeed, and gently push you when you get stuck. The right community can mean the difference between burnout and breakthrough.

Whether you're building a business, managing a household, raising children, or caring for aging parents, having support helps you carry the weight. In this chapter, we'll explore how to build a network that fuels resilience, restores energy, and reminds you: you don't have to do it alone.

1. The Role of Community in Work-Life Harmony

When life feels heavy, isolation can creep in. A strong community lightens the load by offering three essentials:

- **Emotional Support:** People who "get it" can help you release stress and feel understood.

- **Perspective & Insight:** Others can spot solutions you might overlook.

- **Accountability:** Trusted peers remind you to honor your goals and boundaries.

One solo entrepreneur put it best:

"When I'm reclaiming my identity and priorities, I need someone non-judgmental, someone forgiving and understanding. A person who helps me see the good, reminds me of what I've survived, and helps me calm the chaos."

For her, community wasn't dozens of people. It was her children, one accountability partner, and a few trusted friends who allowed her to be both *driven and drained*. That's the power of having the right circle of people around you.

2. Engaging with Like-Minded Individuals

Start by identifying the kind of support you need: Are you seeking professional advice? Emotional connection? Help with the day-to-day?

Here's how to begin:

- **Professional Support:** Join LinkedIn communities or organizations like the National Association of Women Business Owners (NAWBO).

- **Emotional Connection:** Try local or virtual groups such as the Moms in Business Association (MIBA) or Boss Moms.

- **Practical Assistance:** Use platforms like Care.com or neighborhood Facebook groups.

Quick Tip: Choose spaces that align with your values, not just your goals. Being seen and accepted matters more than sheer numbers.

3. Nurturing Support Networks

Community isn't just built, it's cultivated. Show up, give back, and stay open to growth. Even at work, you can deepen connections by asking for collaboration or consistent check-ins:

How to strengthen your network:

- **Participate Consistently:** Attend meetings, contribute, follow up on shared goals.

- **Offer Help:** Share expertise, time, or presence

- **Stay Curious:** Ask questions, seek feedback, and allow yourself to evolve through the experience.

One dual-career woman shared how she decided to stop silently struggling and instead spoke up to her manager by saying, "I'm not asking for less work. I'm asking for more meaningful collaboration and consistent check-ins."

Harmony sometimes starts by deepening the connections you already have.

4. The Power of Community on Mental Well-Being

Support isn't just a feel-good bonus; it's a mental health lifeline. Meaningful relationships boost resilience, lower stress, and improve life satisfaction.

Having a solid community can provide:

- **Safe Spaces:** Environments where you can share without fear of judgment.
- **Confidence Boosts:** Having others around that remind you of your strength(s).
- **Perspective:** Strong connections help you reframe challenges and celebrate progress.

One woman shared how empty nesting left her feeling unanchored.

"I had never lived alone before. I moved from my parents' home to marriage to motherhood. Suddenly, the house was quiet, and I didn't know what to do with that."

Her breakthrough came not by filling the silence, but by reframing it:

"I started focusing not on what I had lost, but on what I had created: two thriving, independent children. That gave me joy."

When we process life changes in community, even virtually, we shift from feeling *empty* to feeling *expanded*.

Lessons from Audrey's Story: From Isolation to Empowered Action

Audrey, an elementary school teacher with a dream of launching an educational consulting business, was on the verge of burnout. Between lesson planning, grading, meetings, and family responsibilities, building something for herself felt impossible. Shadows of doubt crept in. She began to wonder if her dream was realistic.

She was running on empty, emotionally and physically, and starting to doubt whether her dream was even realistic.

One night, after scrolling on social media with a migraine and a stack of ungraded papers, she joined an online teacherpreneur group. That single decision changed everything.

Inside the group, Audrey found:

- **Practical Advice:** Time-blocking strategies, course creation tips, and ways to prevent burnout.

- **Emotional Support:** Encouragement when self-doubt and imposter syndrome surfaced.

- **Accountability:** Feedback on pitches, website copy, and celebrating her first client.

The group provided more than just guidance; it held space for the messy, complex reality of her life. Within a year, Audrey began mentoring others, transforming from someone questioning every move she made into a confident woman.

Here's the takeaway: The right community doesn't just offer advice, it restores confidence, amplifies progress, and reminds you: you're never alone.

Empowering Through Shared Learning

Community is more than encouragement; it's shared momentum. When women come together, we teach, listen, challenge, and grow.

A strong network offers:

- **Shared Resources:** Practical tools or shortcuts that make life easier.

- **Learning Opportunities:** Real stories spark real change.

- **Mentorship:** Guidance can arrive in a text, voice note, or casual conversation.

Even small exchanges, a new project management tool, a clever tip for managing family logistics, can create meaningful shifts when it's rooted in empathy and shared experience.

Sustaining Support for the Long Haul

A community thrives when nurtured. Show up for others and yourself.

How to keep it alive:

- **Stay Active:** Regular check-ins, chats, or meetups.

- **Invest Time:** Support isn't transactional; it's relational.

- **Embrace Growth:** People and seasons change. Needs evolve.

When Audrey attended monthly meetings and mentored newer members in the group, she didn't just find support-she became it. Showing up with intention grew her confidence and her impact.

REFLECTION QUESTIONS

1. What part of your life needs support right now?

2. How can you contribute more meaningfully to your network?

3. Who could you reach out to today for guidance and accountability?

ACTIONABLE
Steps

1. **Identify Your Needs:** Clarify what type of support will make the biggest difference: emotional, practical, or professional.

2. **Join a Group:** Find a space that aligns with your values and energy.

3. **Show Up Consistently:** Engagement builds momentum and trust.

A Final
THOUGHT

For the sake of counterargument, here are two statements I've heard women make in the past about having a trusting and supportive community.

"Support looks different for every woman." Sometimes it's a meme at 2 a.m., a quick check-in, or just being seen and heard.

"My family and friends aren't my village anymore." We all change. It doesn't mean that your current relationships are broken or damaged; it means you're transitioning. It's time to build your bridge from where you are and where you want to go. Start rebuilding:

- Establish meaningful interactions with one like-minded person.

- Join a group prioritizing growth over perfection.

- Keep a journal with the mantra: *"I am still becoming. I am not alone."*

Your tribe is out there. Reach for it. Open up. Start small. Community isn't just what you join, it's what you create, one courageous step at a time.

8

Refine, Align, and Shine: Adjust for Challenging Times

"Success is not final, failure is not fatal: It is the courage to continue that counts."
- Winston Churchill

Reevaluate, Realign, Reignite

Work-life harmony isn't a one-time achievement; it's a living, breathing practice. Just like running a business, it requires check-ins, course corrections, and a willingness to pivot. Life will shift, and your plans or strategies must change with it.

This chapter will help you define success on your own terms, assess your current situation, and adjust your approach so that your vision for harmony evolves into the life you want to live.

Define What Success Looks Like to You

Work-life harmony is personal. There is no one-size-fits-all formula or tried-and-true recipe.

Reflect on these questions:

- **What does an ideal workday look like?**
  Structured? Flexible? A mix of focus and spontaneity?

- **How do I feel when I'm in harmony?**
  Energized? Present? Calm?

- **What are my non-negotiables?**
  Responsibilities or moments that must be protected to feel grounded?

Your answers create your unique blueprint for harmony.

Measure What Matters

Business success is tracked through metrics, but harmony is felt. Consider the following questions:

1. **Energy Levels**-Are you constantly drained or genuinely energized?

2. **Emotional Well-being**- Are you calm and content, or anxious and reactive?

3. **Time for Personal Priorities**- Are relationships, hobbies, and health being nurtured?

4. **Work Productivity**
   Meeting goals without burnout?

5. **Feedback from Loved Ones**

   Do those close to you feel connected or shut out?

6. **Business Growth vs. Personal Fulfillment**-Is one thriving while the other suffers?

If you recognize you have low energy or persistent stress in any of these categories, that is your signal to readjust.

Boundaries: The Secret Sauce

Boundaries aren't about saying "no" to others-they're about saying "yes" to your priorities.

Why they matter:

- They protect your time, energy, and peace.
- They build trust and respect when communicated clearly.
- There will be initial discomfort as your habits shift.

"Boundaries can sometimes strain relationships when others aren't used to them, but that doesn't mean they aren't worth setting. The discomfort often means a shift is happening, one that ultimately benefits both parties in the long run." – Leah Katz, Ph.D.

Expect pushback:

- Resistance or guilt from others.

- Feeling "selfish" for saying no.

- Initial discomfort as habits shift.

Realign with Intention

When life shifts, your systems should too. Look out for the following:

- **Spot the Bottlenecks**
  Too many commitments? Poor boundaries? Unrealistic expectations?

- **Reinforce Boundaries**
  End work at a set hour and silence notifications. Time is sacred.

- **Delegate and Outsource**
  Stop doing it all. Hire support. Free up time so you have space for what only you can do.

- **Build Buffer Zones**
  Incorporate time cushions between tasks and transitions.

- **Revisit Self-Care** Sleep, enjoyable activities, and mental clarity are non-negotiable.

- **Lean on Your People**
  Ask for help, communicate your needs, and let others show up.

Embrace the Growth Mindset

Harmony isn't static-it evolves.

- Be **Curious**: Every challenge is a teacher.
- Be **Flexible**: If one method fails, try another.
- Be **Proud**: Small progress beats chasing perfection.

Having the right mindset sets the stage, but seeing it in action makes it real. Growth isn't just about ideas, it's about the choices you make every day. Dana's story shows how one woman created an intentional pathway to realign her life, honor her priorities, and bring her work and personal worlds into harmony. Her journey showcases key principles we've discussed: curiosity, flexibility, and celebrating progress over perfection. These values aren't just theory; they're practical tools you can use to reclaim your time, energy, and focus.

Dana's Story

Dana, a creative entrepreneur and mom of two, was excelling until her growing business began consuming her life. Missed recitals, late-night work, and exhaustion became routine. After missing her daughter's school performance, Dana knew it was time for a change.

Here's her approach:

1. **Redefined Her Priorities**-Presence with her children, creative freedom, consistent self-care.

2. **Assessed the Imbalance**- Saying "yes" too often, working outside boundaries.

3. **Made Strategic Adjustments**- Enforced work hours, hired a virtual assistant, started "Family-First Fridays," and reserved mornings for personal creative projects.

The result? Dana regained her energy, focus, and joy. Clients respected her time, her children had her attention, and her creativity flourished.

REFLECTION QUESTIONS

- What does work-life harmony look like for me?

- Which part of my life feels most misaligned right now?

- What's one small change I can make this week to restore harmony?

Key Takeaways

- Evaluate energy, emotions, time, and feedback regularly.

- Adapt intentionally as life changes.

- Protect your time. Boundaries are self-respect in action.

- Delegate to free up bandwidth.

- Keep evolving. Progress beats perfection.

ACTIONABLE
Steps

1. **Reflect**: Name what's working and what's not.

2. **Choose One Adjustment**: Reinforce a boundary, include time buffers, or outsource a task.

3. **Track Your Progress**: Do weekly check-ins on your energy and emotions.

FINAL THOUGHTS: You Hold the Power

Harmony is a living practice. Boundaries may cause discomfort, but discomfort signals growth. Like Dana, you can shift from chaos to clarity by designing a life rooted in your values.

Ask difficult questions. Make small intentional changes. Show up with joy.

Because the truth is, you already have everything you need. Now is your moment to realign, reignite, and thrive.

Reference

Katz, L. (2021, August 10). *When Boundaries Backfire*. Psychology Today. https://www.psychologytoday.com/us/blog/and-thrive/202108/when-boundaries-backfire

9

Your Path, Your Pace: Find Harmony and Embrace

"Do not go where the path may lead, go instead where there is no path and leave a trail."
- Ralph Waldo Emerson

Reflecting on the Journey

A Moment to Pause

We've arrived at the final chapter. Take a deep breath. Not just physically, but for your mind and heart. Reflect not only on the words you've read, but on the intention behind them.

Work-life harmony isn't a fixed destination. It's a living, evolving commitment. It's a promise to yourself that your career, relationships, and personal goals can coexist and support each other. This is your journey to live fully, intentionally, and on your own terms.

What We've Explored Together

1. The Power of Harmony

Balance isn't about splitting your time evenly. It's about alignment. Harmony means your life feels purposeful, energized, and fulfilling. When you embrace it, you:

- Reduce stress and emotional burnout
- Boost mental and physical well-being
- Gain clarity, focus, and fulfillment

Prioritizing harmony isn't indulgent; it's a sustainable way to live, work, and lead.

2. Practical Strategies That Work

Throughout this book, we explored habits that create lasting harmony:

- Setting boundaries that protect your energy
- Practicing mindfulness to stay grounded
- Delegating and saying no to make room for what truly matters

These aren't one-time fixes. They are tools to return to, adjust, and refine as your life evolves.

3. The Power of Productivity Tools

Technology should serve you, not the other way around. Tools like Trello, Asana, ClickUp, Google Calendar, and other automation apps can help you:

- Protect your priorities
- Free up mental space
- Focus on what fulfills you most

Productivity isn't about doing more. It's about creating room for what matters.

4. The Strength of Community

Harmony doesn't happen in isolation. When you surround yourself with people who share your values, you:

- Gain accountability
- Learn through shared experiences
- Grow through encouragement and support

Your tribe reminds you that you are not alone, and your goals are valid.

FINAL THOUGHTS:
Choose Progress Over PERFECTION

There's no perfect version of work-life harmony, only what works for you. Some seasons will demand more of your work and time; others will call you to relax, rest, and reconnect. That's not failure. That's life.

Here's what matters:

- **It's Your Path**: Define harmony in a way that's true to you.
- **It's Your Pace**: Tiny, steady steps create major shifts.
- **It's Your Journey**: Give yourself grace, adjust as needed, and most importantly, keep moving forward.

Your Call to
ACTION

This book isn't just words on a page; it's an invitation to act. Today, choose one small step:

- Set a meaningful boundary

- Reach out to someone who supports you

- Download a tool to organize your appointments or support your productivity.

- Take 10 minutes to journal, reflect, or do mindfulness.

Don't wait for the "right time." **Now is the right time.**

It's Your Time

You've read. You've reflected. And now you're ready to live it.

- Embrace your unique definition of harmony.

- Walk boldly toward the life you're creating.

- Leave breadcrumbs of inspiration for others who are ready to follow.

This isn't the end. It's a new beginning. You already have what it takes.

You're not behind.
You're not too late.
You're exactly where you need to be.

The Harmony Within

You've taken a brave step, recognizing the fact that growth isn't always comfortable, but it's necessary. Each challenge you face will stretch, mold, and call you to rise in ways you may not think possible.

The power of a growth mindset lies in persistence. It's not about being perfect; it's about being open to learning, trying again, and becoming the version of yourself who no longer survives but thrives.

Before we move forward, I invite you to pause and think about where you are in your own journey. Do you need to shift from resistance to readiness, choose curiosity over fear, or have joy over discouragement?

If you've been nodding along while reading, thinking to yourself, *"I know what I need to do, but I need the structure and support to actually do it,"* that one thought is the reason why I have created the PRONE to Power framework. Keep reading because in the last few pages of this book, I give you a glimpse into this system I have created and used myself for over a decade.

Let's take everything you've learned and translate it into action, your action. The following pages are here to help you pause, look inward, and begin applying the PRONE Method to your real, everyday life. Because harmony starts within, and the more you nurture it, the more it will ripple outward into your work, your relationships, your legacy.

Harmony in Action

A Self-Reflection Guide for Women Ready to Thrive
Guided by the PRONE to POWER™ Framework

You've reached the final stretch of *Harmony Hustle* now, it's time to personalize your journey. This section is your opportunity to slow down, reflect, and intentionally apply the PRONE principles to your everyday life.

What is PRONE?

The PRONE Method is a mindset shift and success framework for sustainable work-life harmony.

- **P – Priorities**
  Focus on what matters most, not just what's urgent.

- **R – Rejuvenate**

  Protect your peace and energy through rest and restoration.

- **O – Organized**

  Structure your time, tasks, and space to support your goals.

- **N – Navigate Boundaries**

  Set and uphold boundaries that honor your well-being.

- **E – Empowerment**

  Own your choices, voice, and vision.

PRONE to Harmony: REFLECTION PROMPTS

PRIORITIES

- What are the top three priorities in your life right now?
- How do they show up in your current schedule or routine?
- What needs to shift to bring them to the forefront?

REJUVENATE

- What activities help you recharge physically, mentally, or emotionally?
- How can you make time for those practices each week?

ORGANIZED

- Where do you feel disorganized or scattered at work or at home?
- What system, tool, or habit could help bring more clarity or flow?

NAVIGATING BOUNDARIES

- Where are you overextended or saying "yes" when you mean "no"?

- What boundary needs to be created or reinforced in your life?

- How can you express that boundary with confidence and clarity?

EMPOWERMENT

- Where are you shrinking, settling, or holding back?

- What bold move do you need to make to step fully into your power?

Harmony Check-In

- What does a harmonious day look and feel like for you?

- Imagine your ideal flow. What's happening? Who's there? How do you feel?

Write your Harmony Commitment Statement:

"I commit to creating work-life harmony by…"
(Revisit this whenever you feel pulled in too many directions.)

Your Harmony Is Just the Beginning

You made it to the end, but really, this is the beginning.

One of the biggest challenges my clients face isn't knowing what to do; it's staying consistent long enough to see results. That's where the **PRONE to POWER™: Accountability Hour** comes in. Twice a month, you'll have a focused, supportive space to plan, act, and reflect. No fluff, no wasted time, just the accountability you need to make harmony your new normal.

In that hour, you won't just move forward, you'll strengthen your consistency, build confidence, and stay grounded.

Together, we commit. We follow through. We build momentum because growth is inevitable when accountability is present.

READY TO
take the next
STEP?

Visit https://calendly.com/sacolalehr

to schedule a 30-minute pressure-free conversation,
and let's start resetting your work-life rhythm together.

WHAT'S
Next?

If this book spoke to you, if it encouraged, inspired, or empowered you, I'd be so grateful if you'd take a moment to leave a review on Amazon. Your words may be the encouragement another woman needs to start her own journey toward harmony.

Let's keep the conversation going:

Email me: SaCola@SaColaLehr.com

Tune in: *Work It, Live It, Own It!* podcast available on all major platforms

Explore more: SaColaLehr.com for more information.

Thank you for reading, for showing up, and for investing in yourself. I appreciate you more than you know.

www.ingramcontent.com/pod-product-compliance
Lightning Source LLC
Chambersburg PA
CBHW020739130626
46554CB00006B/2050